Do you KNOW Your HUSBAND?

by Dan Carlinsky

D1166194

Published by Sourcebooks, Inc.
P.O. Box 4410, Naperville, Illinois 60567-4410
(630) 961-3900
FAX: (630) 961-2168
www.sourcebooks.com

Library of Congress Cataloging-in-Publication Data

Carlinsky, Dan.
Do you know your husband? / by Dan Carlinsky.
p. cm.
ISBN 1-4022-0199-0 (alk. paper)
1. Men. 2. Man-woman relationships. I. Title.
HQ801 .C27756 2004
305.31—dc22
2003020060

Think you know all about the man on the other side of the dinner table? Well, maybe. Let this little book be the judge.

The fact is, no matter how long you've been together, there's probably plenty you don't know about the man in your life. If the two of you are like most couples, you probably talk more about the neighbors and the news than about yourselves. The result: an information gap.

Counselors say that knowing about your partner's past and preferences can be important—even things like "Who was his best friend in grade school?" and "Does he hate squash?" Knowing, they say—even knowing such bits of trivia—is a sign of caring.

Now, that's not to say that if you and he are on the verge of a split, knowing his shoe size will save your relationship. But, as the lady said as she offered chicken soup to the dying man, "It couldn't hurt!"

So grab a pencil and show what you know. The answers, of course, are not in the book; only he can say. So after you've completed the test, ask him to check your answers and figure your score.

The test has 100 questions. Count ten points for each correct answer. Where you miss some of a multi-part question, divide and take partial credit; you'll need all the help you can get. Here's how to rate yourself:

Above 900: Very impressive. In fact, downright amazing.

700-900: Pretty good, but you might want to work a little to polish off your knowledge. Start asking questions...and pay attention.

Below 700: Weak. Ask him to give you a remedial course.

Take the "Do You Know Your Husband?" test. You may find you have something to brag about, or you may be humbled. Either way, just by going over your answers together, you'll learn a little and have some fun as well. Good luck.

—D.C.

1. FOR STARTERS, WILL HE TAKE THIS TEST:

___ Eagerly?

___ Indifferently?

___ Kicking and screaming?

2. DOES HE HAVE HIS TONSILS?

___ Yes

___ No

3. WHAT DOES HE GENERALLY DO WITH JUNK MAIL?

___ Throw it away without opening it

___ Skim it, just in case

___ Read it carefully no matter what

4. WHAT'S HIS BOSS'S WIFE'S FIRST NAME?

_____

5. IF YOU DIED TOMORROW, HOW SOON WOULD HE WANT TO GET INTO ANOTHER RELATIONSHIP?

___ Right away

___ In a while

___ Never

6. WHICH OF THESE CAN'T HE DO?

_____ Make a decent cheese omelet

_____ Do "walk the dog" with a yo-yo

_____ Juggle three oranges

_____ Sing the national anthem without missing a word

7. IF YOU SAY "CROSS YOUR LEGS," WILL HE:

_____ Cross them at the ankles?

_____ Cross them at the knees?

_____ Put one ankle on the other knee?

8. CAN YOU NAME AT LEAST ONE OF HIS OLD FLAMES—FIRST AND LAST NAME?

_____

9. WHAT'S HIS SHOE SIZE?

_____

10. HOW DOES HE PUT ON SHOES AND SOCKS?

_____ A sock and a sock, then a shoe and a shoe

_____ A sock and a shoe, then a sock and a shoe

11. WHEN WAS THE LAST TIME HE SPOKE—ON THE PHONE OR IN PERSON—WITH ONE OF HIS RELATIVES? WHICH ONE?

_____

12. DOES HE THINK HE'S MORE GENEROUS WITH:

_____ Time?

_____ Money?

13. WITHIN FOUR POUNDS, HOW MUCH DOES HE WEIGH?

_____

14. WOULD HE LIKE TO RIDE INTO SPACE?

_____ He'd love it!

_____ Are you kidding?

15. HOW MANY PAIRS OF GLOVES OR MITTENS DOES HE OWN?

_____ None

_____ One

_____ Two

_____ Three or more

16. DOES HE KICK LEFT-FOOTED OR RIGHT-FOOTED?

_____

17. IN WHICH POCKET DOES HE USUALLY CARRY HIS WALLET?

_____

18. AND HOW MANY PHOTOS DOES HE KEEP IN IT?

_____

19. WHERE WAS HIS FATHER BORN?

_____

20. WHAT'S HIS MOTHER'S TELEPHONE NUMBER?

_____

21. IF SOMEONE BROUGHT HIM TO A CASINO AND GAVE HIM A PILE
OF CHIPS, WHERE WOULD HE TAKE THEM?

_____ To a card game

_____ To the roulette table

_____ To the craps table

_____ To the cashier, to turn them in for money

22. ASSUMING HE LIKED THE LOCATION, WOULD HE RATHER HAVE:

_____ A one-week vacation at a luxury hotel?

_____ A two-week vacation at a just-decent hotel?

23. WHAT ARTICLE OF CLOTHING DID HE BUY FOR HIMSELF MOST RECENTLY?

_____

24. WHICH OF THESE FILMS HAS HE SEEN?

_____ Gone with the Wind

_____ Star Wars

_____ Casablanca

_____ Frankenstein

25. DOES HE BELIEVE IN AN AFTERLIFE?

_____ Definitely

_____ Definitely not

_____ He's uncertain

26. WHICH ONE OF YOUR WOMEN FRIENDS DOES HE FIND MOST ATTRACTIVE?

_____

27. IN A DENTIST'S WAITING ROOM, WHICH WOULD HE PICK UP?

_____ A health magazine

_____ A travel magazine

_____ A news magazine

_____ A sports magazine

_____ None; he'd rather stare at the wall

28. IF HIS FAIRY GODMOTHER OFFERED HIM ANY CAR IN THE WORLD, WHICH WOULD HE CHOOSE? (TWO BONUS POINTS IF YOU KNOW THE COLOR TOO.)

_____

29. DID HE HAVE ANY PETS AS A CHILD?

_____ Yes, a _____ named _____

_____ No

30. WHICH PARTS OF THE NEWSPAPER DOES HE READ REGULARLY?

_____ Front page

_____ Sports

_____ Business

_____ Comics

_____ Advice column

_____ Obituaries

_____ Other

_____ He doesn't often read a newspaper

31. ON VACATION IN AN AREA HE'S NEVER BEEN TO BEFORE, WHICH WOULD HE HEAD FOR FIRST?

_____ A museum

_____ A historic site

_____ A sports arena

_____ Someplace else: _____

32. CAN HE RAISE ONE EYEBROW AT A TIME?

_____ Yes

_____ No

33. HE'S WALKING DOWNTOWN. HE GLANCES AT THE SIDEWALK AND DISCOVERS A WAD OF PAPER MONEY. WHAT DOES HE DO?

_____ Pocket it

_____ Look around for a store where he can buy himself something

_____ Start thinking about a gift for someone else

_____ Call the police to ask if someone reported lost money

34. FOR WHOM DID HE VOTE IN THE LAST BIG ELECTION?

_____

35. DOES HE CONSIDER SHOPPING FOR BIRTHDAY, ANNIVERSARY, OR HOLIDAY CARDS:

_____ A pleasure?

_____ Pure drudgery (but he does it)?

_____ Something for you to do?

36. YOU'RE IN AN INTIMATE FRENCH RESTAURANT FOR DINNER.
THE MENU OFFERS ONLY TWO CHOICES FOR EACH COURSE.
WHICH DOES HE PICK?

_____ Pâté or _____ fresh melon

_____ Onion soup or _____ vichyssoise

_____ Duck in orange sauce or _____ steak in pepper sauce

_____ Chocolate mousse or _____ lemon soufflé

37. WHAT'S HIS SHIRT SIZE?

_____ Neck

_____ Sleeve

38. WHAT'S HIS BELT SIZE?

_____

39. WHO CUTS HIS HAIR? (IF HE HAS NO HAIR, SMILE AND TAKE
YOUR TEN POINTS FOR FREE.)

_____

40. DID HE COLLECT ANYTHING AS A CHILD?

_____ Yes, he collected _____

_____ No

41. CAN YOU NAME AT LEAST THREE OF HIS CHILDHOOD NEIGHBORS?

_____

42. HOW MANY TIMES A DAY DOES HE BRUSH HIS TEETH?

_____ Zero

_____ One

_____ Two

_____ Three or more

43. WHAT DOES HE CONSIDER HIS BEST PHYSICAL FEATURE?

His _____

44. DOES HE LOOK AT MEN'S MAGAZINES THAT FEATURE PHOTOS OF NUDE WOMEN?

_____ Often

_____ Sometimes

_____ Never

45. DOES HE THINK SMOKING MARIJUANA SHOULD BE LEGAL?

_____ Yes

_____ No

_____ He's undecided

46. NAME HIS ELEMENTARY SCHOOL.

_____

47. NAME THE PERSON HE CONSIDERS HIS CLOSEST FRIEND.

_____

48. HOW DOES HE USUALLY SIGN HIS NAME?

_____ With his full legal name

_____ With part left out

_____ With one or more initials

_____ With a nickname

49. DOES HE REMEMBER WHERE YOU WENT ON YOUR FIRST DATE TOGETHER?

_____ Yes

_____ No

50. IF HE WON A HUGE LOTTERY PRIZE, WHAT WOULD HE DO?

_____ Quit work

_____ Take time off but intend to return

_____ Keep working

51. WHICH AROUND THE HOUSE CHORE DOES HE DISLIKE MOST?

_____

52. IF YOU GAVE HIM SOME MONEY AND ASKED HIM TO PICK UP
SOMETHING AT THE CLEANER'S FOR YOU, WHAT WOULD HE DO
WITH THE CHANGE?

____ Keep it

____ Give it to you

53. YOU AND HE HAVE JUST BEEN PRESENTED WITH THE BILL FOR
DINNER AT A RESTAURANT. BECAUSE THE WAITER FORGOT TO
WRITE DOWN YOUR APPETIZERS, YOU HAVE BEEN
UNDERCHARGED. WHAT DOES HE DO?

____ Tell the waiter

____ Say nothing and pay the bill

____ Say nothing and leave an
extra tip, figuring the
waiter undercharged
you "as a favor"

55. WHICH IS CLOSEST TO HIS
IDEA OF A FUN EVENING?

____ Watching TV or reading

____ Hanging out with
friends or family

____ Going to a show or
concert

54. HOW DID HE LEARN TO
DRIVE A CAR?

_____

56. WHAT WAS HIS FIRST JOB? (EVEN A PART-TIME JOB HE HELD AS A YOUNGSTER.)

_____

57. HAS HE EVER SHOT WITH A BOW AND ARROW?

_____ Yes

_____ No

58. WHO'S HIS FAVORITE AMONG YOUR RELATIVES?

_____

59. AND HIS LEAST FAVORITE?

_____

60. IN WHICH OF THE FOLLOWING WOULD HE LIKE A FREE LESSON FROM AN EXPERT? (CHECK AS MANY AS YOU THINK HE'D CHOOSE.)

_____ Cooking

_____ Tennis

_____ Scuba diving

_____ Auto repair

_____ Mixing drinks

_____ Cabinet making

_____ Fly fishing

61. WHAT WAS HIS APPROXIMATE GRADE AVERAGE IN HIGH SCHOOL?

_____

62. GIVEN FOUR TV CHANNELS FROM WHICH TO MAKE A
SELECTION, WHAT WOULD HE WATCH?

_____ A football game

_____ A science or technology show

_____ A quiz show

_____ An old movie

_____ None

63. ON A SWELTERING SUMMER DAY, YOU STOP FOR ICE CREAM.
ONLY FOUR FLAVORS ARE AVAILABLE. HE PICKS:

_____ Vanilla

_____ Chocolate

_____ Strawberry

_____ Pistachio

64. HAS HE READ A BOOK IN THE PAST YEAR? TEN POINTS IF YOU
KNOW, AND IF HE DID, FIVE BONUS POINTS IF YOU CAN NAME IT.

_____ Yes, _____

_____ No

65. YOU'RE AT A SMALL GATHERING AT THE HOME OF A FRIEND. AFTER SOME BORING VACATION VIDEOS, THE FRIEND STARTS TO SHOW VERY X-RATED FOOTAGE. WHAT DOES HE DO?

_____ Leave the room

_____ Protest loudly

_____ Stay, with discomfort

_____ Stay, but tell you to leave

_____ Stay and have a great time

66. AND WHAT WOULD HE DO IF YOU WEREN'T THERE?

_____

67. WHAT WOULD HE SAY IS THE MOST COMMON CAUSE OF ARGUMENTS BETWEEN YOU?

_____

68. IN HIS OPINION, WHICH OF YOUR FRIENDS HAVE DONE THE WORST JOB OF CHILD RAISING?

_____

69. DOES HE EVER WALK AROUND THE HOUSE NUDE WHEN NO ONE ELSE IS THERE?

_____ Yes

_____ No

70. DOES HE THINK HE KEEPS A SECRET WELL? (FORGET WHAT YOU THINK. WHAT'S HIS OPINION?)

____ Yes

____ No

71. WHICH HABIT OF YOURS MOST ANNOYS HIM?

_____

72. HOW DOES HE FEEL ABOUT HIS MIDDLE NAME? (OR, IF HE DOESN'T HAVE ONE, HOW DOES HE FEEL ABOUT NOT HAVING ONE?)

____ Likes it

____ Hates it

____ He's neutral

75. DOES HE KNOW THE BIRTHDAY OF AT LEAST ONE OF YOUR RELATIVES?

____ Yes

____ No

73. WHO WILL HE SAY IS THE FUNNIEST PERSON HE KNOWS?

_____

74. HE'S WALKING, IN NO PARTICULAR HURRY. ACROSS THE STREET, HE SEES A CROWD AND TWO POLICE CRUISERS WITH LIGHTS FLASHING. DOES HE:

____ Cross over to find out what's happening?

____ Keep walking, glancing back over his shoulder?

____ Ignore the whole incident?

76. HAS HE EVER HAD STITCHES? IN WHAT PART OF THE BODY?

_____ Yes, _____

_____ No

77. DOES HE DRINK PLAIN WATER DURING THE WORKDAY?

_____ A lot

_____ Now and then

_____ Never

78. IS HE SUPERSTITIOUS? WHICH OF THESE DOES HE FEAR, EVEN A LITTLE?

_____ Friday the 13th

_____ Black cats

_____ Broken mirrors

_____ Spilled salt

_____ Open umbrellas indoors

_____ None of these

79. HE PULLS INTO A METERED PARKING SPACE. THERE ARE EIGHT MINUTES REMAINING ON THE METER. HE'S PLANNING A TEN-MINUTE ERRAND. WHAT DOES HE DO?

_____ Put in a coin to be safe

_____ Put in no money and try to rush through the errand

_____ Put in no money and not worry about it

80. WHEN WAS THE LAST TIME HE WROTE A PURELY PERSONAL LETTER OR EMAIL TO ANYONE?

_____ No more than a few days ago

_____ About a week or so ago

_____ A month ago, at least

_____ A year or more ago

81. WHICH STATEMENT BEST EXPRESSES HIS POINT OF VIEW ABOUT WHETHER THE MOTHERS OF YOUNG CHILDREN SHOULD TAKE A PAYING JOB?

_____ "They should work outside the home if they like."

_____ "They shouldn't unless the money is really needed."

82. WHAT STYLE FUNERAL WOULD HE WANT?

_____ Large, formal

_____ Small, informal

_____ None

83. DOES HE HAVE ANYTHING STASHED AWAY THAT WAS GIVEN TO HIM—BY YOU OR ANYONE ELSE—THAT HE REALLY CAN'T STAND?

_____ Yes, a _____

_____ No

84. WHAT'S HIS FAVORITE SEASON?

____ Spring

____ Summer

____ Fall

____ Winter

85. "I COULD BE REASONABLY HAPPY EARNING 25 PERCENT LESS THAN I NOW EARN." WILL HE AGREE OR DISAGREE?

____ Agree

____ Disagree

86. AMONG YOUR REGULAR ACQUAINTANCES, WHICH COUPLE WOULD HE LEAST LIKE TO SPEND A LONG WEEKEND WITH?

_____

87. WHAT DOES HE THINK ABOUT THE POSSIBILITY OF INTELLIGENT LIFE ON OTHER PLANETS?

____ Very likely

____ Possible, but not likely

____ Out of the question

____ He has no idea

88. CAN HE TOUCH HIS ELBOWS TOGETHER BEHIND HIS BACK?

_____ Yes

_____ No

89. WITH 1 BEING VERY CALM AND 5 BEING VERY HIGH-STRUNG, HOW NERVOUS DOES HE CONSIDER HIMSELF?

_____ 1

_____ 2

_____ 3

_____ 4

_____ 5

91. SINCE THE AGE OF 18, HAS HE THROWN WATER ON A FULLY CLOTHED PERSON?

_____ Yes

_____ No

90. "ORGANIZED COMPETITIVE SPORTS ARE BAD FOR KIDS BECAUSE THEY OVEREMPHASIZE WINNING." WHAT'S HIS VIEW?

_____ Agrees

_____ Disagrees

_____ Wouldn't give a simple yes or no

_____ No opinion

92. IF HE LEARNED FROM A VERY RELIABLE SOURCE THAT A CLOSE FRIEND'S WIFE WAS CHEATING ON HIM, WHAT WOULD HE DO?

____ Tell the friend

____ Write him an anonymous note

____ Confront the friend's wife

____ Confront the "other man"

____ Ask your advice

____ Do nothing

93. HOW DOES HE GENERALLY GO TO SLEEP?

____ On his back

____ On his stomach

____ On his left side

____ On his right side

94. IF A SERIOUS FIRE BROKE OUT WHILE HE WAS AT HOME, WHAT OBJECT OR OBJECTS WOULD HE TRY TO SAVE FIRST?

_____

95. DOES HE EVER PRAY BY HIMSELF?

____ Yes

____ No

96. DOES HE KNOW HIS OWN ZODIAC SIGN?

_____ Yes

_____ No

97. HE HAS USED A DICTIONARY IN THE PAST SEVEN DAYS—
TRUE OR FALSE?

_____ True

_____ False

98. HOW DOES HE TRIM HIS TOENAILS?

_____ With clippers

_____ With scissors

_____ With a file

_____ By picking them

99. IN HOW MANY LANGUAGES CAN HE COUNT FROM ONE TO FIVE?

_____ 1

_____ 2

_____ 3

_____ 4 or more

100. DOES HE EVER SAY "I LOVE YOU" TO ANYONE BESIDES YOU?

_____ Yes, to _____

_____ No

WHAT <u>DON'T</u> YOU KNOW ABOUT HER?

A Quiz about the Woman in Your Life

Do you KNOW Your WIFE?

Dan Carlinsky